The Illustrated Guide to

TEACHER CREDIBILITY

DOUGLAS FISHER
NANCY FREY
DOMINIQUE SMITH

Illustrations by TARYL HANSEN

CORWIN
Fisher & Frey

CORWIN

FOR INFORMATION:

Corwin
A SAGE Company
2455 Teller Road
Thousand Oaks, California 91320
(800) 233-9936
www.corwin.com

SAGE Publications Ltd.
1 Oliver's Yard
55 City Road
London EC1Y 1SP
United Kingdom

SAGE Publications India Pvt. Ltd.
Unit No 323-333, Third Floor, F-Block
International Trade Tower Nehru Place
New Delhi 110 019
India

SAGE Publications Asia-Pacific Pte. Ltd.
18 Cross Street #10-10/11/12
China Square Central
Singapore 048423

Vice President and Editorial Director: Monica Eckman
Senior Director and Publisher, Content and Product: Lisa Luedeke
Associate Product Manager, Content and Product: Sarah Ross
Product Associate, Content and Product: Zachary Vann
Production Editor: Nicole Burns-Ascue
Copy Editor: Diane DiMura
Typesetter: C&M Digitals (P) Ltd.
Proofreader: Theresa Kay
Indexer: Integra
Cover and Interior Designer: Gail Buschman
Marketing Manager: Megan Naidl

ISBN 978-1-0719-8192-4

torn paper images: iStock.com/fongfong2

The Illustrated Guide to TEACHER CREDIBILITY

CONTENTS

online resources

Visit the companion website at
https://companion.corwin.com/courses/Teacher_Credibility
for downloadable resources.

PUBLISHER'S ACKNOWLEDGMENTS

Corwin gratefully acknowledges the contributions of the following reviewers:

Lydia Bagley
Literacy Support Specialist/RtI Facilitator, Cobb County School District
Marietta, GA

Alisa Barrett
Director of Instruction, Greenfield Exempted Village Schools
Greenfield, OH

Shannon Bussey
Principal, Freese Elementary, San Diego Unified School District
San Diego, CA

INTRODUCTION

It started with a question: ***Why do some strategies work better for some teachers than others?*** Or more specifically, why is it that three teachers can implement the same strategy, lesson plan, or instructional materials, and have a different impact on students' learning? Let's say that three different teachers all agree that they are going to use a certain graphic organizer. And let's say that they all understand the tool to be used and provide very similar lessons for students. Why is it that some classes learn more than others? Our search for an answer led us away from a focus on the quality of the lesson plan, strategy, or instructional materials to a focus on the credibility each teacher had with students. Teachers who were more credible with their students had a much higher impact on their learning.

QR Code 0.1: Students talk about credible teachers
qrs.ly/abg86s7

TEACHER CREDIBILITY DEFINED

"The dynamic of teacher credibility is always at play."[1]

Teacher credibility is the perception by students about their teacher's competence, dynamism, trustworthiness, and immediacy.[2] A student's ability to learn is influenced by whether the source (the teacher) is believed to be knowledgeable (competent), enthusiastic (dynamic), reliable (trustworthy), and accessible (immediate). In other words, learning is governed by the social and emotional perceptions that lie just below the surface. We have seen too many teachers implement what should have been effective instructional strategies, but they did not get the impact they hoped for.

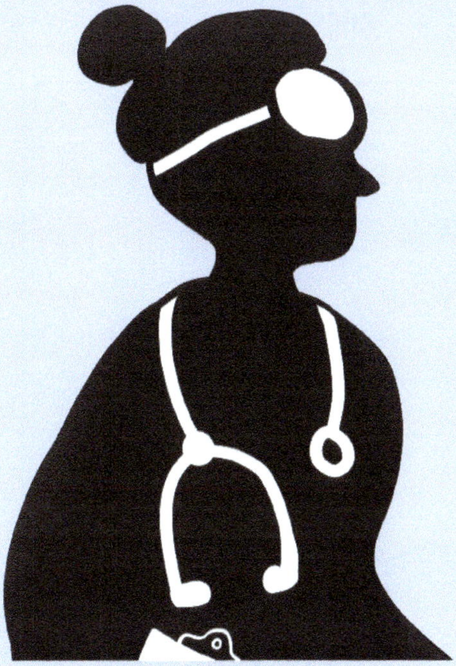

Teacher credibility is sometimes confused with the concept of ***authority***. Being authoritarian does not build credibility. And simply asserting yourself as an authority will not ensure that students learn at high levels. We've all met people who clearly are experts, authorities as it were, in an area. But if we did not trust them, if they were not dynamic and willing to share, and if we did not feel a connection with them, we probably did not give them much of our attention and may even have disregarded what they said. The medical field calls this *bedside manner*; in education, it is called ***teacher credibility***.

Importantly, teacher credibility differs from teacher–student relationships, which are also important. Teachers and students should have healthy, growth-producing relationships, in part because students learn more when these are present, and they are more likely to take risks knowing that the classroom is safe. It's hard to imagine that a teacher could be credible with students without a strong relationship. But teacher credibility extends to other areas, specifically trust, competence, dynamism or passion, and immediacy or perceived closeness.

An effect size is a measure of the impact of a specific influence on learning. John Hattie (2023) summarized more than 450 influences. The average of all influences is **0.40**, thus ***those over 0.40 have the potential to accelerate learning.***

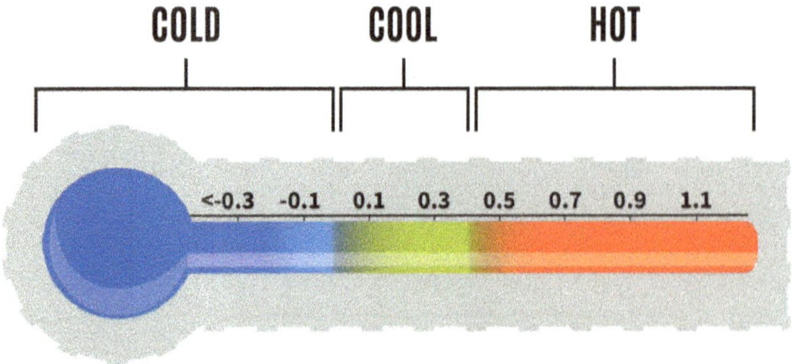

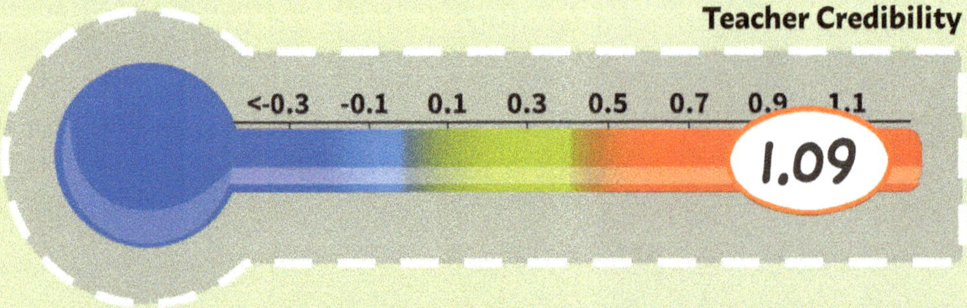

The effect size of teacher credibility is noteworthy: 1.09. In fact, teacher credibility is one of the most influential aspects of the teaching and learning process. And it's one that we can choose to improve.

When a teacher is *not* perceived as credible, students tune out. They fail to show up; they fail to complete tasks; they fail to engage with peers; they fail. And quite frankly, we can't afford for students to do so. We need students to engage, to trust their teachers, and to choose to participate in their learning. The four aspects of teacher credibility—trust, competence, dynamism, and immediacy—can help do just that.

Consider the following success criteria that will be the focus of this illustrated guide:

- ☐ I can develop routines and procedures that ensure that trust is maintained so that students know we have a healthy, growth-producing relationship that allows them to take risks in their learning.
- ☐ I can demonstrate my competence using familiar routines and acknowledge new learning, building students skills as they develop confidence in their own learning.
- ☐ I can create a dynamic learning environment in which students see value in their learning knowing that I care deeply about them and their learning.
- ☐ I can find ways to maintain immediacy with students, ensuring that I am relatable and vulnerable.
- ☐ I can support others in developing and maintaining their credibility.

In this book we focus on the four dimensions of teacher credibility and provide actionable ways that you can maintain and improve your students' belief that they can learn from you. We offer several tools and ideas, all illustrated for ease of access, so that you can maximize the impact you have on your students. And some day, those students will return and ask you, *"Do you remember me?"* and you will because you had a profound impact on their development.

QR Code 0.2: Teachers talk about credibility
qrs.ly/r2g86sf

Notes on...

INTRODUCTION

SECTION 1

TRUST

Trust: ***noun.*** **\'trəst**

1: assured reliance on the character, ability, strength, or truth of someone or something.

2: one in which confidence is placed.

QR Code 1.0:
Trust Discussion
qrs.ly/2egneur

Students need to know that their teachers really care about them as individuals and have their best academic and social interests at heart. Students also want to know that their teachers are true to their word and are reliable. Students need to trust their teachers. And this goes in all kinds of directions. For example, students want their teachers to be honest. Lying to a student damages trust. Of course, there are topics that are off-limits, but not being truthful reduces credibility. Students know when their work is not stellar and wonder why we say it is. They see it in our faces when we refuse to answer a question.

But trust is more than truthful responses.

It's also about healthy, growth-producing relationships. Strong student-teacher relationships make it safe for students to take academic risks. When the relationships are strong, and students know what to expect from their teachers, they are more likely to ask for help, share their ideas, and try to do hard things. Students want to know that you care and that you will support them to meet and exceed their expectations. They want predictability in their relationship with their teachers and value the mentorship you provide.

A simple definition of trust involves truth and reliability of information. But when it comes to complex organizations like schools, the definition of trust is more complex. We have adopted the following definition of trust: "**Trust is an individual's or group's willingness to be vulnerable to another party based on the confidence that the latter party is benevolent, reliable, competent, honest, and open.**"[1] This definition acknowledges that we must be vulnerable if we are to develop trust. And that goes for students as well as our professional peers. But for now, we will focus on trust between students and teachers.

Annette Baier, a New Zealand philosopher, made an interesting observation about trust when she wrote, "*We inhabit a climate of trust as we inhabit an atmosphere and notice it as we notice air, only when it becomes scarce or polluted.*"[2] Trust becomes obvious when it is scarce. As educators, we need to ensure that trust is not scarce or polluted, because this damages our credibility and thus student learning. Trust should be in the air, all around students, so that they can learn. To accomplish this, we need to attend to five elements:[3]

5 ELEMENTS OF TRUST

Benevolence: Confidence that one's well-being or something one cares about will be protected by the trusted party. Assurance that others will not exploit one's vulnerability or take advantage even when the opportunity is available.

Honesty: The trusted person's character, integrity, and authenticity. Acceptance of responsibility for one's actions. Not distorting the truth in order to shift blame to another.

Openness: The extent to which relevant information is shared. Openness signals reciprocal trust.

Reliability: Consistency of behavior so that others know what to expect. Others have a sense of confidence that their needs will be met in positive ways.

Competency: The ability to perform as expected and according to standards appropriate to the task at hand.

BASICS FOR BUILDING TRUST

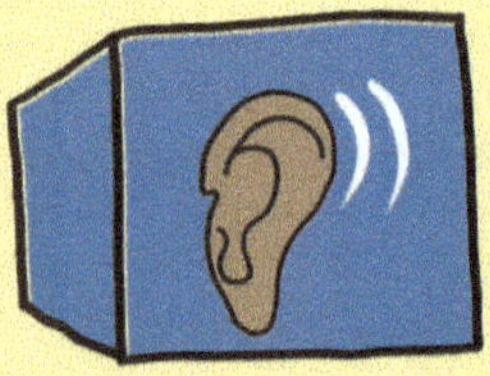

LISTEN

Provide students a chance to explain, especially when they make mistakes academically or behaviorally. Consider what students say before making the next decision. Dismissing, ignoring, or embarrassing a student will compromise their trust.

SHOW APPRECIATION

Students who feel recognized by teachers generally respond in positive ways. Students want to be noticed and valued. Praise for their actions goes a long way in building trust. And specific praise builds their competence.

SHARE RESPONSIBILITIES

Students appreciate being asked to be responsible for some aspects of the class operation and organization. It shows that you trust others with important tasks and you earn trust in return. Showing you trust your students is a sure way for them to trust you.

SHOW FAIRNESS

For many students, fair is about getting the same as everyone else. Adults recognize that this is not the necessarily the case, but students expect teachers to be fair. When there is a need to differentiate, teachers should offer general explanations and ensure that students are receiving the support they need.

QR code 1.1: Classroom talks about fairness qrs.ly/z3g86sj

A MEASUREMENT OF TRUST

If you want to get a sense of the level of trust in your classroom or school, you can use the *Student Trust in Faculty Scale*.[4] This tool is very brief, which makes it useful for student administrations. The goal of the tool is to "capture student perceptions and recollections of teacher behavior, which allow for judgments to be made about their relative openness, benevolence, reliability, competence, and honesty" (p. 264).

Data are powerful but need to be used wisely. Focusing on trust is much like studying the roots of a plant. Without care, the examination can damage or destroy the very thing you are trying to learn about.[5]

Before you collect these data, ask yourself these questions:

- ***What is our purpose for gathering these data?***
- ***What is the scope of the data collection?***
- ***Who will gather the data? By when?***

WHAT

- WHO?
- WHEN?

WHY

- PURPOSE?
- SCOPE?

HOW

- WHAT CAN I LEARN?
- HOW CAN I INCREASE MY TRUSTWORTHINESS?

After you have the data collected, ask yourself these questions:

- ***What did I learn about trust in my classroom or school?***
- ***How can I increase my trustworthiness with students?***
- ***What can I learn from my colleagues about trustworthiness?***

It is important to administer this assessment confidentially so that trust is maintained. Students should be told that their participation is voluntary and that they will suffer no penalty for not completing the survey. They should also be told that they may skip any items they are uncomfortable answering. *The scoring directions are in the* ***appendix***.

STUDENT SURVEY

Directions: Please tell us how much you agree or disagree with each of the statements about your school by filling in the bubbles on the right, choosing from (1) Strongly Disagree, (2) Disagree, (3) Neither Agree nor Disagree, (4) Agree, or (5) Strongly Agree.

		Strongly Disagree				Strongly Agree
1.	Teachers are always ready to help.	①	②	③	④	⑤
2.	Teachers are easy to talk to at this school.	①	②	③	④	⑤
3.	Students learn a lot from teachers in this school.	①	②	③	④	⑤
4.	Students at this school can depend on teachers for help.	①	②	③	④	⑤
5.	Teachers at this school do a terrific job.	①	②	③	④	⑤
6.	Teachers at this school really listen to students.	①	②	③	④	⑤
7.	Teachers always do what they are supposed to do.	①	②	③	④	⑤
8.	Students are well cared for at this school.	①	②	③	④	⑤
9.	Teachers at this school are good at teaching.	①	②	③	④	⑤
10.	Teachers at this school are always honest with me.	①	②	③	④	⑤

Source: Adams & Forsyth (2009).

TAKE ACTION

If you, or you and your colleagues, want to take action based on the data collected and analyzed, consider the 6 steps of action planning.

1. **Set a reasonable and measurable goal.** What do you want to accomplish and by when?
2. **Identify tasks.** What steps will be required to reach the goal?
3. **Prioritize tasks.** We tend to identify too many tasks and get overwhelmed. Which of the tasks will yield the most useful results?

6. **Monitor and revise.** Reality will hit and you may need to revise the plan. When you monitor the tasks and their impact, you'll know when to revise.
5. **Set deadlines.** Create a timeline that you can follow. Don't expect immediate success, but note the completion of each milestone.
4. **Allocate resources.** What will it take, in terms of time, effort, or money, to complete the tasks?

7. **Celebrate!** Too often, we forget to recognize our accomplishments. Achieving a goal is cause for celebration and will build our individual and collective efficacy.

REGAIN TRUST WHEN IT HAS BEEN DAMAGED

Trust is easier to gain than regain. Thus far, we have focused on creating and maintaining trust. But sometimes trust is violated or broken and needs to be rebuilt. Some of the ways that trust can be rebuilt include the following:

Apologize. When you make a mistake, own it and apologize. Yes, especially to students. We are all human and we all make mistakes. An apology can go a long way toward rebuilding trust.

Listen. When trust has been broken, it is time to listen more intently. You have to learn where the hurt lies so that you can address that hurt. Recovery begins with acknowledgment. Sometimes, students need time to vent. If you broke trust with students, they will need some time to vent to move past the hurt. Of course, you are still the adult, and there are parameters about student conduct. You may want to invite a colleague to mediate the conversation.

Make amends but not promises you cannot keep. Your goal is to make things right, but in doing so, don't make the problem worse by making a promise you can't keep. Amends can come in a range of ways, from direct approaches such as fixing physical damage to indirect approaches such as providing time.

Allow time. As the saying goes, "Time heals all wounds." Sometimes, depending on the damage done, you might need a light touch with a student or group of students. Don't shy away from them, but recognize that it may take some time for them to trust you again.

Be reliable. Once trust is violated, it is human nature to look for additional evidence that the person is not trustworthy. Redouble your efforts to be reliable. Follow through on your promises.

Forgive yourself. As we noted before, we are human and, as such, fallible. But sometimes we forget to forgive ourselves. That is not to say that we ignore the consequences of our actions, but rather that we come to terms with them and learn to forgive.

QR code 1.2: Teacher meets with student to repair relationship
qrs.ly/34g86sk

USE TRUST TO BUILD TEACHER–STUDENT RELATIONSHIPS

To paraphrase the late educator Rita Pierson, young people don't learn from old people they don't like.

In addition to our collective personal knowledge about the power of humane, growth-producing relationships, there is compelling research evidence to support this. We have already noted that teacher credibility has an effect size of 1.09, which is impressive. But if we just consider teacher–student relationships, the effect size is 0.47, still above average and likely to further accelerate learning. There is a distinction between teacher credibility and teacher–student relationships. The former operates in one direction and lies within the student's perceptions. The latter is bidirectional, as both teacher and student participate in its development. These are not unrelated to one another, and in fact trust is foundational in relationships.

> *Positive relationships between teachers and students are among the most commonly cited variables associated with effective instruction. If the relationship is strong, instructional strategies seem to be more effective. Conversely, a weak or negative relationship will mute or even negate the benefits of even the most effective instructional strategies.*[6]

The Search Institute has created a Developmental Relationships Framework. Their model has five major components (expressed from the perspective of an individual student):

1. **Express care**—Show me that I matter to you.
2. **Challenge growth**—Push me to keep getting better.
3. **Provide support**—Help me complete tasks and achieve goals.
4. **Share power**—Treat me with respect and give me a say.
5. **Expand possibilities**—Connect me with people and places that broaden my world.

Search INSTITUTE

The Developmental Relationships Framework

Young people are more likely to grow up successfully when they experience developmental relationships with important people in their lives. Developmental relationships are close connections through which young people discover who they are, cultivate abilities to shape their own lives, and learn how to engage with and contribute to the world around them. Search Institute has identified five elements—expressed in 20 specific actions—that make relationships powerful in young people's lives.

Elements	Actions	Definitions
Express Care Show me that I matter to you.	**Be dependable**	Be someone I can trust.
	Listen	Really pay attention when we are together.
	Believe in me	Make me feel known and valued.
	Be warm	Show me you enjoy being with me.
	Encourage	Praise me for my efforts and achievements.
Challenge Growth Push me to keep getting better.	**Expect my best**	Expect me to live up to my potential.
	Stretch	Push me to go further.
	Hold me accountable	Insist I take responsibility for my actions.
	Reflect on failures	Help me learn from mistakes and setbacks.
Provide Support Help me complete tasks and achieve goals.	**Navigate**	Guide me through hard situations and systems.
	Empower	Build my confidence to take charge of my life.
	Advocate	Stand up for me when I need it.
	Set boundaries	Put limits in place that keep me on track.
Share Power Treat me with respect and give me a say.	**Respect me**	Take me seriously and treat me fairly.
	Include me	Involve me in decisions that affect me.
	Collaborate	Work with me to solve problems and reach goals.
	Let me lead	Create opportunities for me to take action and lead.
Expand Possibilities Connect me with people and places that broaden my world.	**Inspire**	Inspire me to see possibilities for my future.
	Broaden horizons	Expose me to new ideas, experiences, and places.
	Connect	Introduce me to people who can help me grow.

NOTE: Relationships are, by definition, bidirectional, with each person giving and receiving. So each person in a strong relationship both engages in and experiences each of these actions. However, for the purpose of clarity, this framework is expressed from the perspective of one young person.

Note that each of the major components has actions and definitions. For example, one of the actions is to advocate. *Stand up for me when I need it.* This is one of 20 actions, all of which are powerful. Consider each of the factors from the Developmental Relationships Framework. **Use the scale on the right** to estimate the number of students who believe that you demonstrate each factor.

Express care—Show me that I matter to you.

no students ······ few students ······ most students ······ all students

Challenge growth—Push me to keep getting better.

no students ······ few students ······ most students ······ all students

Provide support—Help me complete tasks and achieve goals.

no students ······ few students ······ most students ······ all students

Share power—Treat me with respect and give me a say.

no students ······ few students ······ most students ······ all students

Expand possibilities—Connect me with people and places that broaden my world.

no students ······ few students ······ most students ······ all students

Source: The Developmental Relationships Framework is copyrighted by Search Institute, Minneapolis, MN (www.searchinstitute.org) and used with permission.

Take a look at your responses. What do you notice? What are your strengths and opportunities for growth? Are you willing to share your responses with a trusted peer and solicit advice?

TAKE ACTION

Using the action plan process, what is your goal for improving or maintaining positive, growth-producing relationships with students?

FOSTERING HEALTHY, GROWTH-PRODUCING RELATIONSHIPS

Some of the ways that we have seen teachers develop healthy, growth-producing relationships with students include these:

Knowing their names and how to pronounce them. This may seem obvious, but students often report that their teachers don't know their names. Make a commitment to learn all your students' names. Make sure you pronounce their names correctly as well.

Say hello and good-bye to every student every day. There are any number of ways to do this. Looking at each student and greeting them conveys that the student is valuable and worth your time. Some teachers invite students to choose their greetings, such as a handshake, high-five, or hug (if allowed in the district). Others stand at the door and greet each student as the student enters the room. We find that more teachers say hello individually than good-bye.

Speak with respect. Again, this may seem obvious, but we have lost count of the number of times we have heard harsh or sarcastic words come from a teacher. It damages relationships and prevents students from bonding with the adult who is there to teach them. *Your words are powerful.*

QR code 1.3: Teacher greets students by name qrs.ly/sjg86sm

Know their interests and attend extracurricular events. Students will play harder, dance better, and sing louder when you are in the audience. You are a superhero, and they are thrilled when you are present at their events. We have lost count of the number of times a student finished a game or performance and ran up to a teacher, asking the teacher to meet their parents. We also notice that students whose parents can't attend stand proudly next to their teachers. Remember to attend events that are outside of your personal interests. Dominique is a big sports fan, but you can also find him visiting the chess club, the anime group, and every play and poetry slam that students are part of.

Monitor nonverbal communication. Estimates are that more than half of our communication is nonverbal. It's not just the words we use with students; it is also our body language. And students are always paying attention to the messages we send. Eye rolls, crossed arms, and defensive stances send powerful negative messages to students about the approachability of an adult and whether this adult is one to trust and value.

Share your world. No, not necessarily your entire personal life, but your world. Young students are surprised to learn that you buy groceries and sometimes even eat out, just like they do. They want to know more about you, and you should share aspects of your life appropriate for school.

We made that seem really easy. And it is. It's a choice.

We can focus our energy on developing relationships with students because we know it matters. Or we can ignore the evidence of the social and emotional dimensions of learning at our own peril.

Simply said, trust matters for students and colleagues, and it is foundational to the relationships we establish. These relationships are a grist for learning. They make it safe for students to take risks and chance being wrong. And they help students develop into productive members of their communities. Yet, they are only part of what makes a teacher credible. Relationships and trust are worth the investment and pay dividends for years, especially when a student returns and asks, ***Do you remember me?***

QR Code 1.4: Strong teacher-student relationships qrs.ly/rzg86sn

Notes on...
TRUST

SECTION 2

COMPETENCE

Competence: ***noun.***
**com·pe·tence | \ 'käm-pə-tən(t)s **

The quality or state of being competent: such as the quality or state of having sufficient knowledge, judgment, skill, or strength (as for a particular duty or in a particular respect).

QR Code 2.0:
Competence Discussion
qrs.ly/vfgneut

"I can learn from this person."

In any learning situation, we hope to find ourselves in good hands. This aspect of teacher credibility is focused on the demonstrated competence of the teacher as perceived by the student. Not surprisingly, perceived incompetence on the part of the teacher significantly undermines teacher credibility. Incompetent teachers "don't care about the course and/or the students" and

> *make tests too hard, are unwilling to help students succeed, and/or present poor lectures. They may bore or confuse students, overload them with information, mispronounce words. . . . These characteristics reflect a basic lack of teaching skills.*[1]

There's actually a name for this in communication research: ***teacher misbehaviors***. There is a significant spillover effect as it relates to perceived incompetence. Teachers viewed as incompetent by students are more likely to be viewed as untrustworthy and uncaring, even when they didn't do anything specifically to undermine relationships with students. An incompetent teacher is quickly assumed by students to be someone they should distance themselves from.

Students want to know that their teachers know their stuff and know how to teach that stuff. They expect an appropriate level of expertise and accuracy from their teachers. Further, students measure competence by the ability of the teacher to deliver instruction that is coherent and organized. They expect that lessons are well paced and include accurate information. Students regularly make decisions about which adults they can learn from and which adults they cannot learn from. In doing so, they make judgments about our competence. They want to know that you "know your stuff" and that you know how to teach that stuff in ways that make sense. Interestingly, students are not looking for 25 different learning strategies to be tried out on them. They want a few that they know and expect from you. When teachers change their strategies too frequently, students wonder if the teacher really knows how to teach.

COMPETENCIES OF TEACHERS

Here's a reasonable list of teacher competencies.[2] Using the "traffic light" scale, identify your strengths across these dimensions.

1. Interacting Well With Students

2. Creating a Learning Environment

3. Good at Lesson Plan Design

4. Able to Use Varied Teaching Strategies

5. Able to Assess

6. Able to Identify Student Needs

7. Good at Communication

8. Able to Collaborate

9. Maintaining a Professional Appearance

10. Demonstrating a Commitment to the Profession

As you read this chapter, think about how students would perceive the competence of their teachers. After all, the evidence says that learning increases when students believe that their teachers are competent.

TAKE ACTION

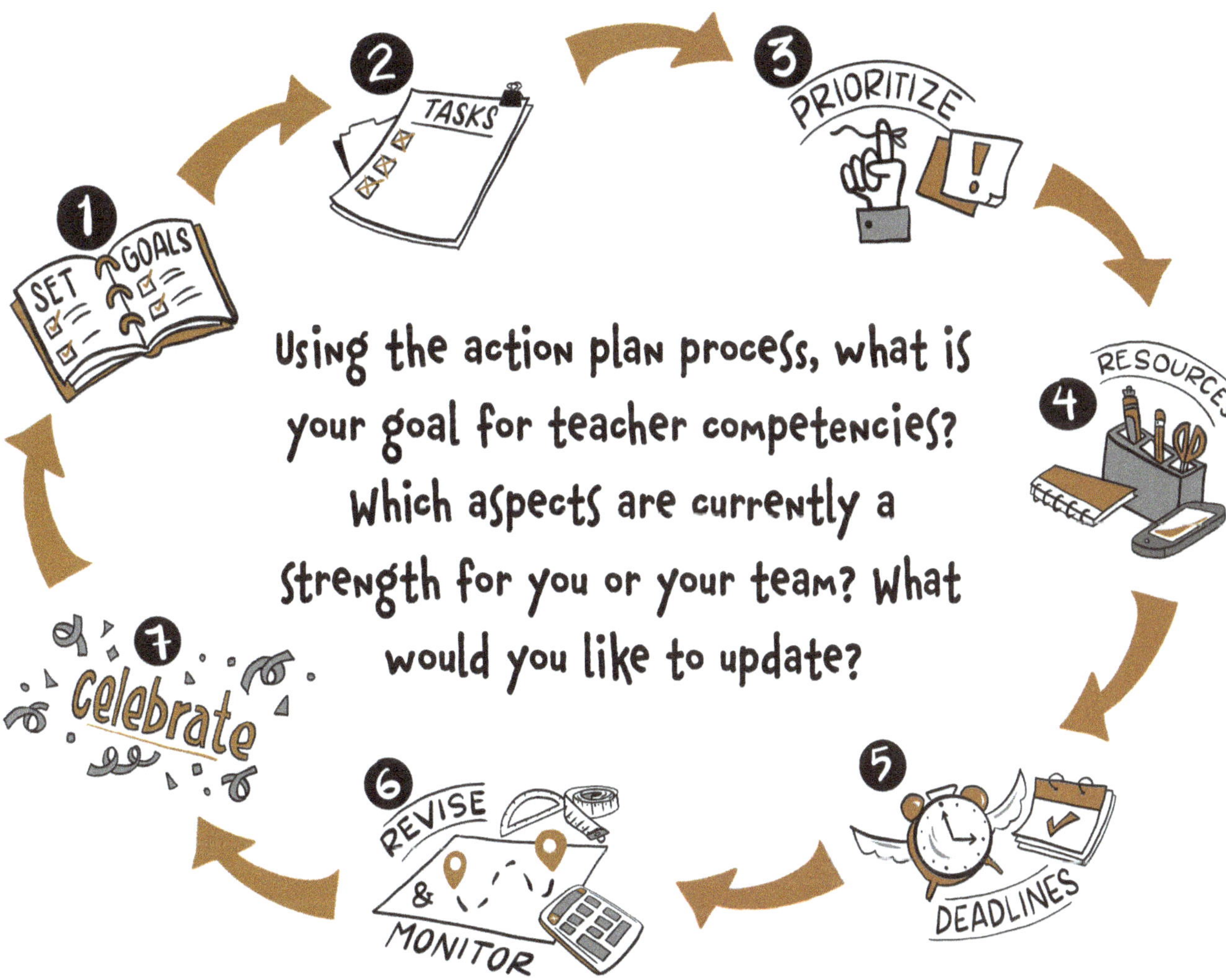

Using the action plan process, what is your goal for teacher competencies? Which aspects are currently a strength for you or your team? What would you like to update?

PEDAGOGICAL CONTENT KNOWLEDGE

Students know when you don't know your subject and when you aren't able to teach it effectively. And when teacher credibility declines, so does learning. Students need a teacher who is more than simply knowledgeable about the subject matter. Students also need a teacher who can teach that subject clearly and effectively. There is a theory that explains this phenomenon—**pedagogical content knowledge**.[3] Teachers should be knowledgeable and know how to teach the content.

First, teachers need to know their content. That may mean that some professional learning time is focused on the content students need to learn. But deep understanding of the content is not enough. We think of content knowledge as necessary but not sufficient. Importantly, there is not one right way to teach things, but there are wrong ways.

Teachers who have strong pedagogical content knowledge are also comfortable when they don't know something. They do not try to hide that fact from students, and they don't invent answers that may or may not be accurate. Instead, they provide honest responses to students when questions are raised for which they are not sure about the answer.

QR Code 2.1: Teacher explains a complex concept
qrs.ly/f8g86ss

TEACHER CLARITY

With an **effect size of 0.85**, there is good reason to consider ***teacher clarity*** as an essential part on one's practice. At a basic level, teacher clarity requires that the teacher know what students need to learn, communicate those learning intentions directly, and ensure that students know what success looks like. At a deep level, teacher clarity extends to the lucidity of the examples and guided instruction the teacher provides, and the practice students are asked to do.

Competent teachers do not spend valuable instructional time on things that students have already learned. Students are frustrated when the teacher squanders time like this, and they question whether the adult can accurately gauge their strengths and needs. Teacher clarity requires that you know what students already know so that you can teach in the gap between what they know and what they need to know.

There are several tools to determine what students already know, such as initial assessments, reviews of performance on previous units, and interactions with students.

Once we know what students need to learn, teachers identify an appropriate sequence of learning. Often called ***learning progressions***, the flow of content is an important consideration. Teachers who cannot logically sequence concepts and skills risks being viewed as scattered, and their students' perception of their competence suffers. As with many things in education, there are likely many appropriate progressions and some bad ones.

Once the sequence of learning has been identified, students need to know each day what they are supposed to learn and how they will know they have learned it. This learning intention (which others might call a *learning target*, *goal*, or *objective*) elevates the level of the students' investment in learning, as it moves them from compliance to commitment. Learning intentions are paired with success criteria. Success criteria equip students with a means for gauging their own learning.

If there is sufficient clarity in the lesson, students will be able to answer these three questions.[4]

1. What am I learning today?
2. Why am I learning this?
3. How will I know that I have learned it?

The first question focuses on the *content being learned*. The second question focuses on the *relevance of the lesson*, and we will spend more time on this topic in the next chapter on dynamism. And the third question focuses on the *success criteria*. Each of these is important if you want to mobilize the power of teacher clarity, not to mention increase your credibility. We suggest that you use these questions as a temperature check. Ask three to five random students these questions, and keep track of the percentage of answers that are correct.

Most of us draw a clear association between something we learned well and the person who taught it to us. When students experience an increased sense of competence in learning, they attribute it in part to the skills of the teacher. The teacher's clarity provides a pathway for students to become more competent. And when they see themselves as competent, you benefit as well. But simply having learning intentions and success criteria does not ensure that the lesson flows. Competence requires that you align instructional events with the learning intentions.

QR Code 2.2: Teacher Clarity using the 3 clarity questions
qrs.ly/5ug86su

QUALITY INSTRUCTIONAL EXPERIENCES

To accomplish the learning intentions and reach the success criteria, there are times in a lesson in which the teacher is doing more of the work and there are times in which the students are doing more of the work. The flow of the lesson depends on students' increased understanding. The goal is to release responsibility to students as quickly as possible, while ensuring that students experience sufficient support and scaffolding to increase their own responsibility for learning. Often called the gradual release of responsibility,[5] high quality instruction requires that teachers plan and organize lessons. Teachers can select from four major categories of instructional strategies that increase students' competence and confidence.

I DO IT!

Focused instruction is a time during which teachers establish the purpose (the learning intentions and success criteria) and provide students input. They open up their brains and talk through their own thinking. Focused instruction is also a time for direct or explicit instruction.

WE DO IT!

Guided instruction scaffolds students' understanding as their teachers use prompts, cues, and questions to address errors and misconceptions. Guided instruction can be done with the whole class, in a small group, or individually.

YOU DO IT TOGETHER!

Collaborative learning requires that students interact with their peers using academic language to share or problem solve. Students are given tasks or prompts that they likely could not complete individually, and teachers structure the interactions.

YOU DO IT ALONE!

Independent learning provides students with opportunities to both practice and apply what they have been taught. This can occur during class time or outside of the class.

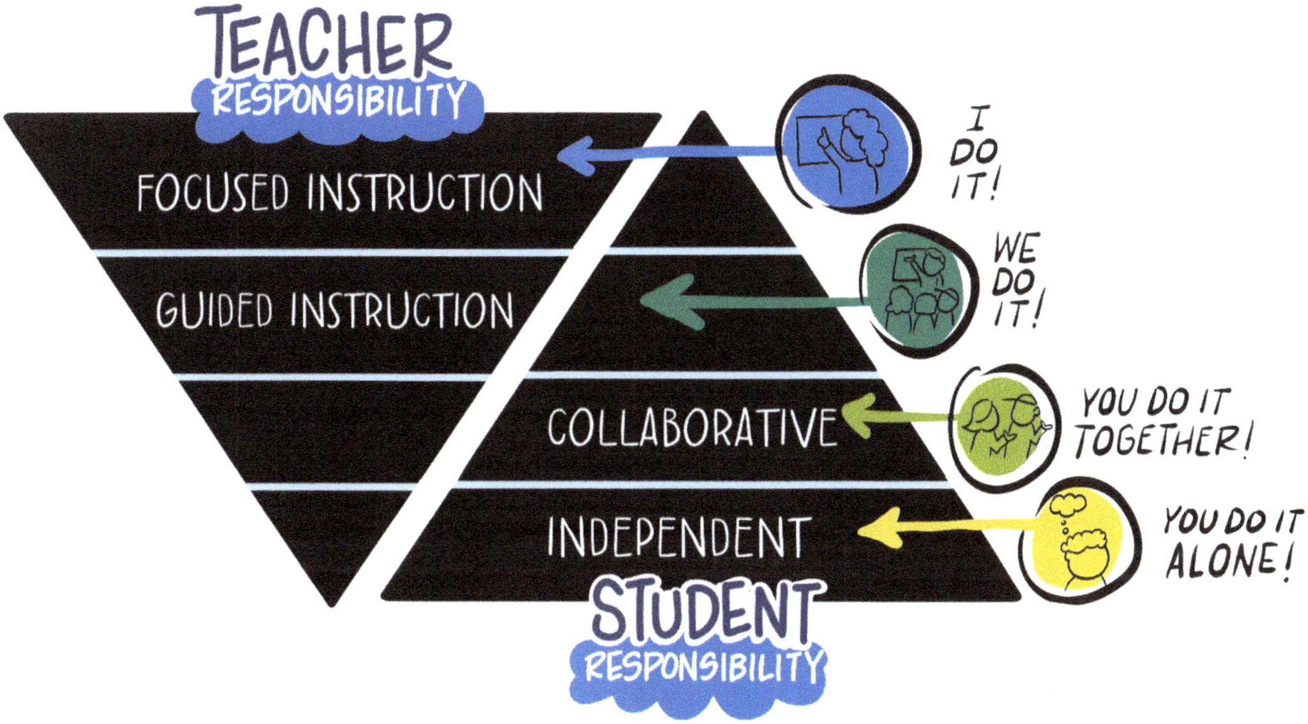

Source: Used with permission of Association for Supervision & Curriculum Development, from *Better Learning Through Structured Teaching: A Framework for the Gradual Release of Responsibility*, Fisher, D. & Frey, N., 3rd edition, 2021; permission conveyed through Copyright Clearance Center, Inc.

The problem with this graphic is that people think we intend lessons to be linear. They're not. you can start at any phase, depending on what you want students to learn.

QR Code 2.3: Gradual release of responsibility
qrs.ly/rjg86sx

FOCUSED INSTRUCTION IN PRACTICE

Indicators of teacher to students, student to peers, and students to the content interaction and engagement during ***focused instruction***.

	TEACHER TO STUDENTS	STUDENT TO PEERS TO PEERS	STUDENTS TO CONTENT
FOCUSED INSTRUCTION ***I do it***	✔ Teacher explicitly states the learning intention(s) for lesson. ✔ Teacher restates learning intention(s) throughout lesson. ✔ Teacher models process and context for thinking. ✔ Teacher invites students to join and attend to modeling. ✔ Teacher poses convergent questions for student response (seeking answer). ✔ Teacher poses divergent question for student response (questions without specific answer). ✔ Student behavior reflects cognitive interaction and engagement. ✔ Teacher revisits other phases of gradual release.	✔ Students explain their reasoning to each other. ✔ Student conversation builds on responses of others. ✔ Students talk to partner about a posed question and explain thinking to each other. ✔ Students explore others' thinking and reasoning through • Restating • Paraphrasing • Questioning ✔ Students continually try to reclarify thinking by explaining reasoning in multiple ways.	✔ Students demonstrate background knowledge. ✔ Students communicate the intended learning intention(s) in their own words. ✔ Students take notes. ✔ Students record using graphic organizer.

QR Code 2.4:
Teacher Modeling
qrs.ly/h5g86sy

GUIDED INSTRUCTION IN PRACTICE

Indicators of teacher to students, student to peers, and students to the content interaction and engagement during ***guided instruction***.

	TEACHER TO STUDENTS	STUDENT TO PEERS TO PEERS	STUDENTS TO CONTENT
GUIDED INSTRUCTION ***We do it***	✔ Teacher poses question and asks partners to think, share, answer, and justify their thinking. ✔ Teacher supports students to develop thinking through • Prompts • Cues • Convergent questions • Divergent questions • Direct explanation (after prompts and cues) ✔ Teacher questions students to uncover misconceptions. ✔ Teacher assists students to clarify their thinking. ✔ Teacher revisits other phases of gradual release.	✔ Students explain their reasoning to each other. ✔ Student conversation builds on responses of others. ✔ Students talk to partner about a posed question and explain thinking to each other. ✔ Students explore other students' thinking and reasoning through • Restating • Paraphrasing • Questioning ✔ Students continually try to clarify thinking by explaining reasoning in multiple ways.	✔ Students are collecting, recording, and interpreting. ✔ Student tasks are visible and directly reflect the purpose in • Reading • Writing (pictures, words, numbers) • Conversation • Solving problems ✔ Students consolidate understanding about concepts they are learning (synthesizing, building learning).

QR Code 2.5: Guided Instruction
qrs.ly/gpg86t3

COLLABORATIVE LEARNING IN PRACTICE

Indicators of teacher to students, student to peers, and students to the content interaction and engagement during ***collaborative learning***.

	TEACHER TO STUDENTS	STUDENT TO PEERS TO PEERS	STUDENTS TO CONTENT
COLLABORATIVE LEARNING ***You do it together***	✔ Teacher provides a challenging collaborative task for students to apply and extend learning. ✔ Teacher poses a challenging problem, task, or situation for students with which to grapple. ✔ Teacher holds students individually accountable for contributing to the learning. ✔ Teacher revisits other phases of gradual release.	✔ Students work in small groups of not more than five students. ✔ Students facilitate each other's learning. ✔ Students dialog about ideas. ✔ Students participate in content talk using academic language. ✔ Students make inferences and explain reasonableness through evidence. ✔ Students explain their options/opinions they thought about and why they chose certain options/opinions. ✔ Students justify their reasoning by using multiple models or data.	✔ Students are collecting, recording, and interpreting. ✔ Students utilize previously learned concepts in a new/emerging way. ✔ Students interact with concepts without a guaranteed outcome (building meaning).

QR Code 2.6:
Collaborative Learning
qrs.ly/3qg86t1

INDEPENDENT LEARNING IN PRACTICE

Indicators of teacher to students, student to peers, and students to the content interaction and engagement during ***independent learning***.

	TEACHER TO STUDENTS	STUDENT TO PEERS TO PEERS	STUDENTS TO CONTENT
INDEPENDENT LEARNING ***You do it alone***	✔ Teacher confers with students to assess understanding and monitor progress. ✔ Teacher establishes purpose for independent work. ✔ Teacher holds students accountable for independent work. ✔ Teacher revisits other phases of gradual release.	✔ Students teach each other what they have learned.	✔ Students reflect on own learning. ✔ Students are collecting, recording, and interpreting. ✔ Students function independently and manage the tasks on their own.

QR Code 2.7:
Independent Learning
qrs.ly/3hg86t6

TAKE ACTION

Using the action plan process, what is your goal for quality instruction? Which aspects are currently a strength for you or your team? What would you like to update?

Notes on... COMPETENCE

SECTION 3

DYNAMISM

Dynamism: ***noun.***
**dy·na·mism | \ ˈdī-nə-ˌmi-zəm **

An energetic or expansionist quality.
The *dynamism* of a natural leader.

QR Code 3.0:
Dynamism Discussion
qrs.ly/migneuv

This dimension of teacher credibility focuses on **the passion teachers bring to the classroom and their content**. It is really about the ability to communicate your enthusiasm for your subject and your students. And it's about developing spirited lessons that capture students' interest. You don't have to dress up in a toga, but you do have to convey deep interest in students' learning and the content you teach. We all have learned things that we didn't intend to learn because of the passion someone else had. Passion is also conveyed every time with talk about a task, assignment, or activity. The presentation of that information says to students, this is cool, or one more thing to endure.

Passion, I See, is Catching

Let's not forget the line from Shakespeare's *Julius Caesar*, "Passion, I see, is catching." When you display your passion for your subject and your students and you make learning relevant, you harness the power of dynamism. Active, fast-paced learning environments in which students are challenged and supported characterize this third aspect of teacher credibility. Dynamism has to do with passion for teaching and learning as well as the ability to ensure that learning is relevant for students. When we think about dynamism as part of teacher credibility, we think of teachers who

- Are energetic and vibrant
- Seem to enjoy teaching and learning
- Are passionate about education as a profession
- Exude self-confidence

Sometimes, when we talk about this aspect of teacher credibility, people tell us that they are shy, or that this is not their personality. We are not saying that you must dress in a toga during the Greek-Roman unit or stand on a desk and bounce around excitedly, unless that is your personality. We are saying that the learning environment should be dynamic, and students should get caught up in the excitement of learning.

> "The best teachers are people who are passionate about their subject and passionate about sharing that subject with others."[1]

DYNAMISM THROUGH ENTHUSIASM

Enthusiasm is arguably the most considered factor in passionate teaching. Teachers who are excited, and display that excitement for students, can motivate learning.

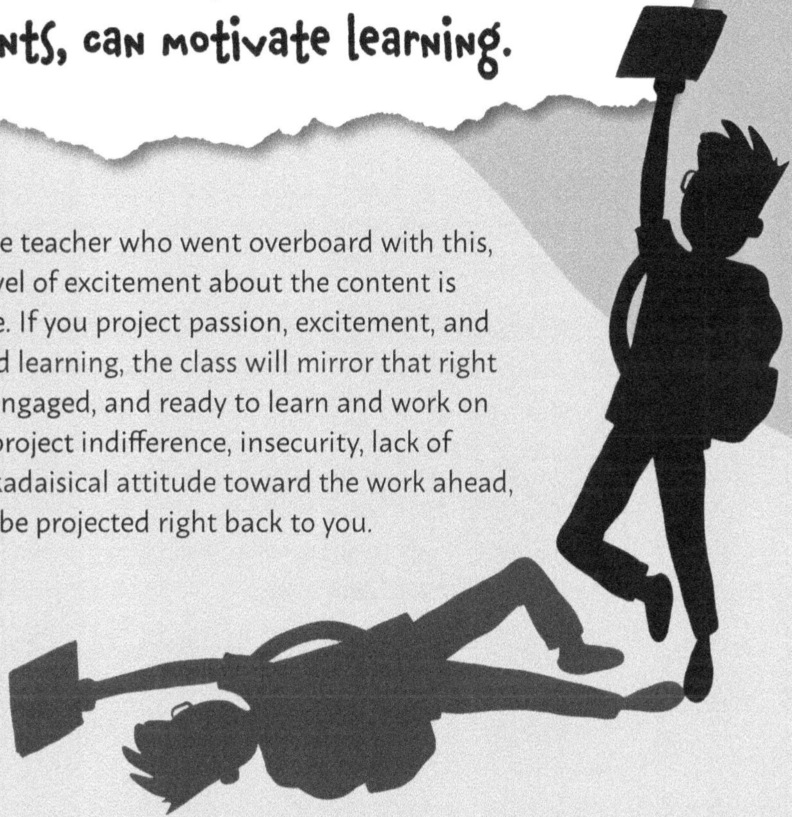

Of course, we've all experienced the teacher who went overboard with this, and we became skeptical. But a level of excitement about the content is useful. Teachers get what they give. If you project passion, excitement, and a sense of urgency for teaching and learning, the class will mirror that right back to you. They will be excited, engaged, and ready to learn and work on something important. But, if you project indifference, insecurity, lack of preparation, or demonstrate a lackadaisical attitude toward the work ahead, those attitudes and behaviors will be projected right back to you.

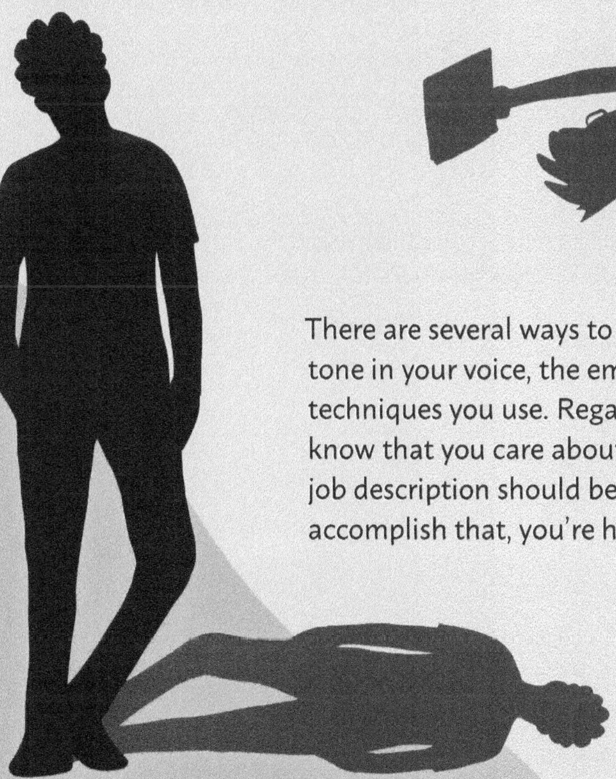

There are several ways to demonstrate enthusiasm, including the tone in your voice, the emotional stories you tell, or the presentation techniques you use. Regardless of the approach, students should know that you care about the content. The first thing on a teacher job description should be to *make content interesting*. If you can accomplish that, you're halfway there.

What is your level of passion for the work you do?

Take the passion inventory. It will help you assess your current level of dynamism and might point to some things that you can do to increase your score, and then perhaps your students' learning.

PASSION INVENTORY

Directions: Score 1 point for each item that depicts you or your students.

1.	I am enthusiastic about my teaching. It is something I enjoy and look forward to doing. It is a fun, exciting, and stimulating activity for me.	
2.	My students can sense my enthusiasm. They have conveyed this impression to me in their evaluations or in their personal comments.	
3.	I am continuing to learn. I am active in research. I read and attempt to keep up with the appropriate literature. I obtain new information from my students.	
4.	My students are witnesses to my interest in learning. They see me doing research, reading the literature, conversing with colleagues, participating in professional conferences, and actively engaging with my discipline.	
5.	I can get absorbed in my work, but not so self-absorbed that others are excluded. I am likely to share what interests me and bring my interests to the attention of others.	
6.	I continue to try new approaches in my teaching. The class that I have taught several times is different and better than when I began. Sometimes I try things that do not work, but these failures do not prevent me from taking new risks or experimenting with my teaching.	
7.	I care about my students. I want them to learn, to realize their potential, and to succeed in class and in other useful and challenging endeavors.	
	Total:	

Source: Wangberg, J. K., Teaching with a passion, American Entomologist, 1996, Volume 42, Issue 4 by permission of Oxford University Press

YOUR SCORE:

7 pts Powerfully passionate!

6 pts Pridefully passionate

5 pts Pretty passionate

<5 pts Seek help from a passion professional!

QR code 3.1: Team reflects on Passion Inventory qrs.ly/ttg86ta

TAKE ACTION

Using the action plan process, what is your goal for displaying passion for students and their learning? Which aspects are currently a strength for you or your team? What would you like to update?

DYNAMISM THROUGH RELEVANCE AND VALUE

There are many things that kill the vibe of a classroom, such as public humiliation of a student, terrible visuals and presentations, monotone presentations, boring tasks, and the like. Students appreciate a cognitive challenge, knowing that their teacher can support their learning. Students also appreciate learning experiences that the teacher is excited about and that are relevant to students. We are not suggesting that teachers simply say, "You'll need this in the real world." Isn't going to school the real world? And being told that you might be able to use this someday in the future is probably not that motivating. Instead, students want to know the answer to the second clarity question that we posed in the previous section: ***Why am I learning this?*** Teachers who exhibit dynamism have no problem with students answering this question and seeing their learning as relevant.

Students want to find value in the tasks they are doing and the content they are learning. When they do, students are much more likely to self-regulate their behavior and focus on the work ahead. Teachers should regularly discuss why students are learning the things they are learning, even "micro-sermonizing" on the value of the content.[2]

In fact, there are at least nine different ways that teachers can share the value of learning with students and questions you can ask yourself to help you design the talking points necessary to ensure that your classroom is a dynamic place in which students want to learn.

QR Code 3.2: Passionate teacher in action
qrs.ly/2qg86tf

9 ASPECTS OF RELEVANCE

UTILITY

- How is what you teach useful?
- How does what you teach allow students to do what they previously would not have been able to do?
- When will students use what you teach?

RELEVANCE

- How does what you teach connect specifically to the real-world interests of at least one of your students?
- What's an interest you know at least some of your students have? How does that link with today's lesson?

SOCIAL STATUS

- How could what your students are learning in your class make the class cooler?
- How could what they're learning redefine "cool"?
- How could what they are learning help them relate to others in new and profound ways?

AUTONOMY

- How does what you teach give students power either now or later in life?
- How is what you teach powerful?

JUSTICE

- How can the work you do in your discipline or art make the world a better, fairer, more just place?
- How can mastery of your discipline or art make it easier to help others?

NOVELTY

- What do most folks not realize about what you teach that if they did realize it would give them a whole different view about why your discipline or art is so good?

ENJOYMENT

- What's fun about what you teach?
- What enjoyment or pleasure do you get from our discipline?

PURPOSE

- How does what your students are learning connect with what it means to be a human being?
- How does what they're learning tap into their deepest desires for their lives—desires to make a difference, to be independent, to be understood?

BEAUTY

- What is beautiful about what you teach?
- How is what you teach beautiful?

Source: Stuart, D. (2023). The will to learn: Cultivating student motivation without losing your own. Corwin.

AVOID BORING INDEPENDENT TASKS

One of the most effective ways to crush dynamism is to hand students a worksheet and ask them to complete it. "Worksheets don't grow dendrites."[3] These "shut-up sheets" may be effective in keeping students quiet and busy, but not learning much. Instead, students need to engage in a variety of tasks, assignments, and activities that deepen their understanding.

But there is a different way to think about the seemingly endless photocopies and workbook pages that teachers use. Consider the worksheet continuum.[4]

THE WORKSHEET CONTINUUM

BUSYSHEET
keeps kids busy but has little educational value

POWERSHEET
directly supports learning; may support other tasks

- word searches; word scrambles; irrelevant coloring, cutting, and pasting
- recall questions; comprehension questions; labeling stuff
- skills practice (only as needed and not for a grade)
- graphic organizers; note-taking templates; data collection tools; planning sheets

Source: Gonzales, Jennifer (2018). Frickin' Packets. Cult of Pedagogy. https://www.cultofpedagogy.com/busysheets/

There are more appropriate tools and less appropriate tools. Not all worksheets are bad. Notice that there are several recommendations toward the "powersheet" end of the continuum. These are likely more useful for students and will probably not harm the dynamism in your classroom. Also, we do believe that students need some skills practice, but these should generally not count for a grade. Remember, practice does not make perfect; practice makes permanent. Of course, students need more than practice; they also need to apply what they have learned in new situations. There are many other tasks and assignments we can give students that do not harm the dynamic learning environment.

WHAT TO DO INSTEAD OF PACKETS

CLASS DISCUSSIONS

- gallery walks
- philosophical chairs
- think-pair-shares

GROUP LEARNING

- jigsaw
- reciprocal learning
- games
- icebreakers
- maker challenges

LONG-TERM PROJECTS

- genius hour
- project-based learning
- service learning

INTERACTIVE EXPERIENCES

- simulations
- role-plays
- labs
- escape rooms

READING AND WRITING

- self-selected reading
- research projects
- journal writing
- short writing challenges
- long-term writing project

PERSONALIZED LEARNING

- HyperDocs
- stations or centers
- listening to podcasts
- blended learning

THOUGHT-PROVOKING LESSONS

- concept attainment
- inductive learning

Source: Gonzales, Jennifer (2018). Frickin' Packets. Cult of Pedagogy. https://www.cultofpedagogy.com/busysheets/

QR Code 3.3: Students engaged in a lab qrs.ly/seg86th

DYNAMISM AND SELF-CONFIDENCE

At this point you might be thinking that being a dynamic teacher sounds great and you are on board with why it matters to your credibility, but you're not sure if you have the self-confidence to pull it off. Your thinking is spot on, as self-confidence is a required element of dynamism, and thus your credibility.

> **self-confidence is what we think we can do and is related to your efficacy, or your belief that you can reach your goals.**[5]

Teachers' beliefs—confidence—about their own teaching abilities impacts how they teach their students. Teachers who have more confidence are more satisfied with their jobs and they are more likely to try out new ideas and innovate with their instruction.[6] The impact on students is notable, with increased achievement and social-emotional growth for students when their teachers are confident.[7]

TIPS FOR INCREASING TEACHER CONFIDENCE[8, 9]

Plan well. When you know what you want students to learn and the tasks, assignments, or activities that will help them learn, you are more likely to deliver these with confidence.

Connect with students. Knowing your students and how they respond to information and ideas, as well as their background knowledge, helps you anticipate the flow of lessons and feel more comfortable when there are questions or challenges.

Cue yourself. Develop verbal reminders, power poses, written affirmations, or wear specific items that remind you that that you have the skills necessary to deliver effective learning experiences for your students.

Phone a friend. Seek ideas, advice, and feedback from other teachers. Share your ideas with others. In doing so, you create a community of professionals, drawing on your collective experiences, and building your collective confidence.

Be kind to yourself. Avoid perfectionism and enjoy the teaching and learning experience. When you make mistakes, which we all do, forgive yourself and move on with the next lesson.

One tool to assess your general feelings about your confidence and self-esteem asks that you consider the following statements, indicating strongly you agree or disagree with each statement.[10]

	STRONGLY AGREE	AGREE	DISAGREE	STRONGLY DISAGREE
1. On the whole, I am satisfied with myself.				
2. At times I think I am no good at all.				
3. I feel that I have a number of good qualities.				
4. I am able to do things as well as most other people.				
5. I feel I do not have much to be proud of.				
6. I certainly feel useless at times.				
7. I feel that I'm a person of worth, at least on an equal plane with others.				
8. I wish I could have more respect for myself.				
9. All in all, I am inclined to feel that I am a failure.				
10. I take a positive attitude toward myself.				

YOUR SCORE:

Items 1, 3, 4, 7, 10 are scored with as follows: Give "Strongly Disagree" 4 points, "Disagree" 3 points, "Agree" 2 points, and "Strongly Agree" 1 point.

Items 2, 5, 6, 8, 9 are reverse scored. Give "Strongly Disagree" 1 point, "Disagree" 2 points, "Agree" 3 points, and "Strongly Agree" 4 points.

Sum scores for all 10 items. The scale ranges from 0–30. Scores between 15 and 25 are within normal range; scores below 15 suggest low self-esteem.

TAKE ACTION

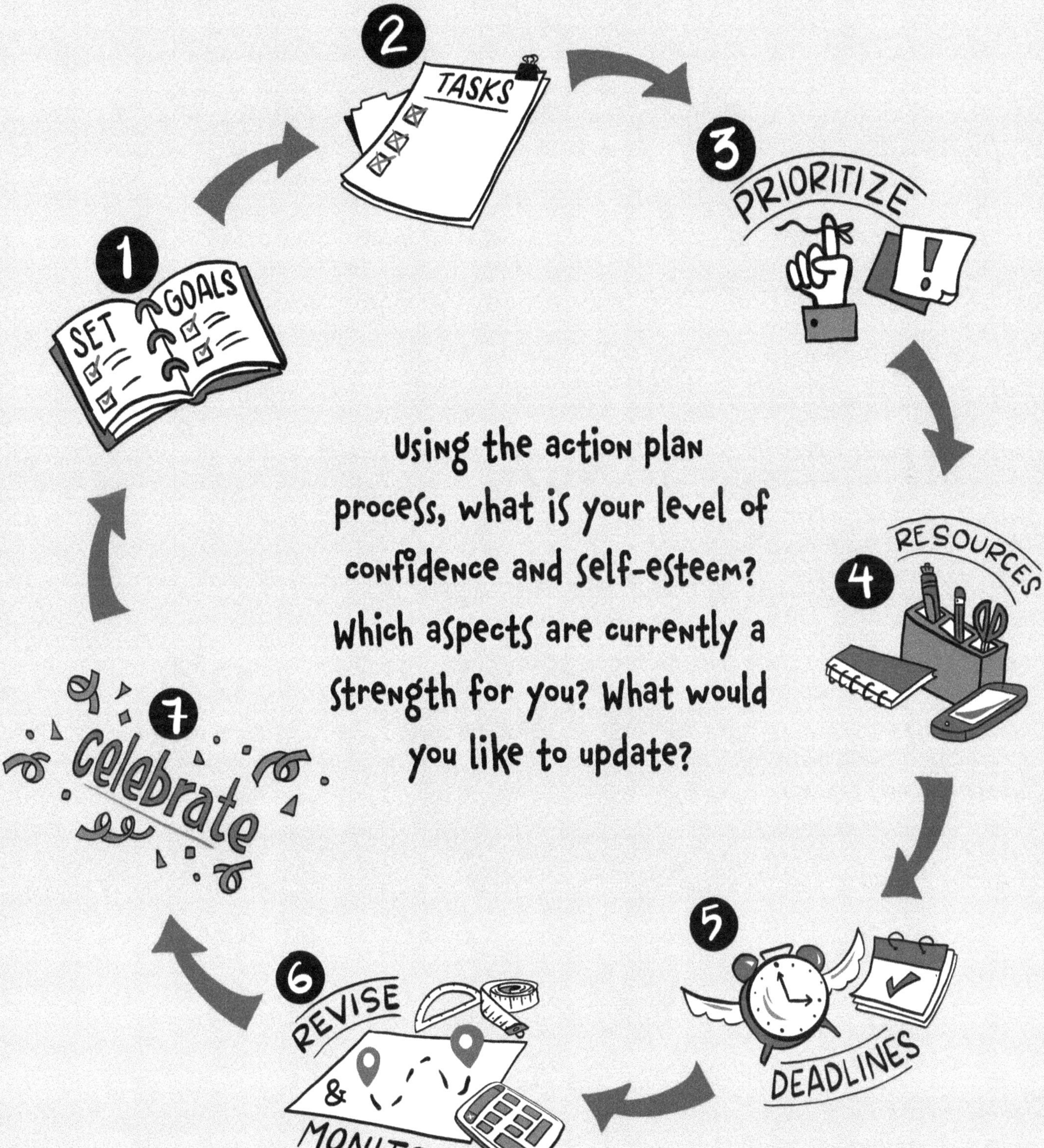

Using the action plan process, what is your level of confidence and self-esteem? Which aspects are currently a strength for you? What would you like to update?

THE IMPACT OF WORRY ON DYNAMISM

One way to strengthening your confidence is keeping your worries in perspective. Worrying constantly will not help you override fear, and it will impede your ability to reflect and change. Worrying drains valuable energy, takes away needed focus, causes fatigue and stress, and steals joy. Worrying is a confidence killer, but it can and should be deliberately controlled. Make a list of the things you have worried most about recently. Keep these worries in mind as you consider the research that follows.

Researchers asked a group of people to identify what worried them and tracked their worries over time. Research on what people worry about revealed that[11]

30%

of the worries concerned things from the past that could neither be changed nor otherwise influenced

40%

of the worries concerned things that never actually happened

12%

of the worries were needless worries about health

10%

of the worries were petty worries about unimportant things

8%

of the worries concerned anything substantial

4%

(1/2 of the 8% substantial issues)

of the substantial worries were things that could be controlled or changed

Highly effective teachers have worries just like the rest of us, but they deliberately refuse to waste their energy stressing over things of which they have no control. Rather, they direct their energy and attention to factors they can control, and they do so with passion, enthusiasm, and determination. Research shows that the best antidote for worry is *purposeful action.*

Engaging in actions that make a difference for others and fearlessly focusing on the work that matters most can help you keep your worries at bay and build the confidence you need to make important decisions that impact students' learning.

So, the next time you find yourself unable to focus or lacking energy and motivation due to worrying, ask yourself if your worries fall into one of the categories listed.

Force yourself to keep things in perspective by understanding that 96% of the things you worry about either will not happen, are out of your control, are needless, or are unimportant in the big picture.

Notes on... DYNAMISM

SECTION 4

IMMEDIACY

Immediacy: *noun.*
im·me·di·a·cy | \ i-'mē-dē-ə-sē,
British often -'mē-jə-sē

1: the quality or state of being immediate

2: something that is immediate—usually used in plural

QR Code 4.0:
Immediacy
Discussion
qrs.ly/2ygneux

Immediacy in psychology is the connection and relatedness between people. Immediacy includes the perceived, and actual distance, between people. "People are drawn toward persons and things they like, evaluate highly, and prefer; and they avoid or move away from things they dislike, evaluate negatively, or do not prefer."[1] Humans engage in both approach and avoidance behaviors often based on the perceived distance between people. Teacher immediacy is highly predictive of teacher effectiveness, at least as perceived by students and classroom observers.[2]

Students want to sense that they are held in high regard and that they are emotionally close to their teachers.[3] Much of this is communicated nonverbally. It's the eye contact that students experience, the nods as they speak, the noticing that we offer. In addition, it's communicated with proximity and verbal language. Teachers who move around the room and are easy to interact with increase students' perception of immediacy. Unfortunately, some students rarely get within three feet of the teacher. Teachers need to be accessible, and yet there needs to be a sense of urgency that signals to students that their learning is important.

Immediacy is all the things that communicate to a student:

I see you, you matter, we are close.

> *High levels of teacher immediacy are correlated with increases in student motivation.*
>
> *"The concept of nonverbal immediacy is based on the idea that teacher nonverbal behavior will promote feelings of arousal, liking, pleasure, and dominance. These feelings are mediated through actions such as eye contact, body position, physical proximity, personal touch, and body movement."*[4]

Importantly, immediacy is a two-way street. "Teachers who perceived their students to be more nonverbally immediate with them in their classrooms expressed more positive affect for the students than did teachers who perceived their students as engaging in less nonverbally immediate behaviors."[5] **The effect size of immediacy is 0.66**, which means that it is likely to accelerate learning.

MEASURING IMMEDIACY

Consider the following examples of general things you can do to ensure that your students feel close to you:

Gesture when talking to the class.

Look at the class and smile while talking.

Circulate around the room.

Call students by name.

Use ***we*** and ***us*** to refer to the class.

Invite students to provide feedback.

Use vocal variety (pauses, inflections, stress, emphasis) when talking to the class.

There is also a tool you can use to assess your immediacy.[6] This can be used as a self-assessment to identify potential areas of strength or need. It can also be used as a tool for others to use to provide perspective. The perspective can be that of students or other visitors to the classroom. We suggest starting with the self-assessment and deciding what you might want to update in the classroom and then, following the change, use the tool to understand the perspective of others. The tool provides a total score (and you can set personal goals to raise your score by increasing some behaviors and reducing others).

QR Code 4.1:
Highlighting immediacy behaviors
qrs.ly/k3g86tp

NONVERBAL IMMEDIACY SELF-REPORT SCALE

Directions: The following statements describe the ways some people behave while talking with or to others. Please indicate in the space at the left of each item the degree to which you believe the statement applies TO YOU. Please use the following 5-point scale:

(1) Never; (2) Rarely; (3) Occasionally; (4) Often; or (5) Very Often.

______ 1. I use my hands and arms to gesture while talking to people.

______ 2. I touch others on the shoulder or arm while talking to them.

______ 3. I use a monotone or dull voice while talking to people.

______ 4. I look over or away from others while talking to them.

______ 5. I move away from others when they touch me while we are talking.

______ 6. I have a relaxed body position when I talk to people.

______ 7. I frown while talking to people.

______ 8. I avoid eye contact while talking to people.

______ 9. I have a tense body position while talking to people.

______ 10. I sit close or stand close to people while talking with them.

______ 11. My voice is monotonous or dull when I talk to people.

______ 12. I use a variety of vocal expressions when I talk to people.

______ 13. I gesture when I talk to people.

______ 14. I am animated when I talk to people.

______ 15. I have a bland facial expression when I talk to people.

______ 16. I move closer to people when I talk to them.

______ 17. I look directly at people while talking to them.

______ 18. I am stiff when I talk to people.

______ 19. I have a lot of vocal variety when I talk to people.

______ 20. I avoid gesturing while I am talking to people.

______ 21. I lean toward people when I talk to them.

______ 22. I maintain eye contact with people when I talk to them.

______ 23. I try not to sit or stand close to people when I talk with them.

______ 24. I lean away from people when I talk to them.

______ 25. I smile when I talk to people.

______ 26. I avoid touching people when I talk to them.

SCORING FOR NIS-S:

Step 1. Start with a score of 78. Add the scores from the following shaded items: 1, 2, 6, 10, 12, 13, 14, 16, 17, 19, 21, 22, and 25.

Step 2. Add the scores from the following items: 3, 4, 5, 7, 8, 9, 11, 15, 18, 20, 23, 24, and 26.

Total Score = Step 1 minus Step 2.

Source: Richmond, V. P., McCroskey, J. C., & Johnson, A. D. (2003). Development of the nonverbal immediacy scale (NIS): Measures of self-and other-perceived nonverbal immediacy. *Communication Quarterly*, 51(4), 504–517. (p. 509).

TAKE ACTION

Using the action plan process, what is your goal for immediacy? Which aspects are currently a strength for you or your team? What would you like to update?

OPTIMIZING YOUR IMMEDIACY

There are effective instructional practices that were useful in creating immediacy. When teachers use these approaches, "The positive relational messages immediacy expresses can reduce students' social anxiety that can interfere with their cognitive processing of class content."[7] Importantly, immediacy cannot compensate for a bad lesson. Instead, immediacy can provide students access to the content and reduce their anxiety, apprehension, and complaints while increasing their feeling of being supported.

1 ***Take advantage of the time before class starts.*** This is an ideal time to talk with students individually and let them know you know them. You can share personal stories or make connections with them about their interests. You can get physically closer to students and greet them individually.

2 ***Get rid of barriers between yourself and your students.*** The number of physical barriers between teachers and students increases as students get older. When teachers sit at a desk, or stand at a podium, lecturing to students, the physical barriers are noticed. Sometimes desks get in the way. Sometimes it's the presentation equipment. One of the ways to remove barriers is to walk around the room rather than standing at a fixed place to deliver information for students.

3 ***Use immediacy behaviors in class discussion to facilitate better outcomes.*** Student-to-student interaction is an important part of quality instruction. In fact, using classroom discussion is one of the ways that teachers can accelerate learning, as it has an above-average impact on learning with an effect size of 0.82. But sometimes class discussions can be difficult to manage, especially when student responses are incorrect or even offensive. When these situations arise, work to ensure that the environment is safe for everyone, and redirect conversations that go astray.

4

Use immediacy to make presentation of information more engaging. In most whole class instructional events, including read-alouds, direct instruction, explanations, demonstrations, and lectures, the visuals used to convey information should be inviting and relevant. Generally, these events should be brief and provide students with an opportunity to interact with the information.

5

Keep your immediacy appropriate and natural. We're not looking for over-the-top performers or "phonies," as the students like to say. Efforts to build immediacy need to be natural and not contrived. We've all been around a person whose eye contact makes us uncomfortable or a person whose gestures are a distraction. Don't let that become you, because your efforts to increase immediacy will not have the desired impact and may actually make things worse. **We're also reminded to go slowly on this one.** Your students are used to a certain style from you, and they value predictability. If you radically change your style, it will be noticed, and you'll probably be thought of as the weirdo rather than an ally. Take your time, and thoughtfully increase your immediacy with students. And then next year, remember that the first day of school is a great opportunity to start out on the right foot.

QR code 4.2: Example of a quality presentation
qrs.ly/qpg86tr

FEEDBACK AND IMMEDIACY

The effectiveness of feedback is impacted by the relationship between people. When there is a stronger sense of immediacy, students are more likely to seek feedback and use that feedback. When immediacy is compromised, students likely hear the feedback as criticism and not as an opportunity to grow and develop.

The **Wise Feedback Model** is designed as an alternative to the compliment sandwich in which teachers give a compliment, an area of improvement, and then another compliment. Too often, students interpret the area of improvement as criticism and not helpful, which interferes with the immediacy between the teacher and student. In that case, they are not sure that the teacher believes that they are capable of meeting high expectations. Instead, providing students with feedback is an opportunity to communicate high expectations, the belief that the student can reach those expectations, and that there are specific steps helpful in reaching the goal.

STEP 1: COMMUNICATE HIGH EXPECTATIONS.

- "I know it feels like this is a very challenging task I'm asking you to do—and it is."
- "Learning how to write a lab report is a new skill that you haven't been asked to do before, but it will help you to think about your skill set as a scientist for when you write your research proposal."
- "Giving a presentation in front of the whole class can feel scary, but it's really good practice for job interviews."

STEP 2: EXPLAIN THAT YOU BELIEVE THE STUDENT CAN MEET THE EXPECTATIONS.

- "Your work to this point demonstrates that you already can do _____ and _____ well."
- "You earned a score of ____ on the last quiz, which shows me that you understand the foundational concepts for the project."
- "Your first draft had some really excellent points, so I know that you are capable of meeting the expectations for the final essay."

STEP 3: PROVIDE ACTIONABLE FEEDBACK THAT DEMONSTRATES SUPPORT.

- "The feedback I gave you on your draft is where you should start as you write the next version—I look forward to reading your final paper!"
- "Looking at your quiz responses, you should start with a review of _____ and _____ concepts so that you feel as comfortable with them as you do with _____, which you did really well on."

Source: Breana Bayraktar, *Tips for Teaching Professors.* higheredpraxis.substack.com

QR Code 4.3: Teacher gives wise feedback
qrs.ly/84g86tt

THE CHALLENGE AND VALUE OF PROXIMITY, VULNERABILITY, AND TOUCH IN DYNAMISM

PROXIMITY

The physical presence of the teacher in the classroom is a powerful motivator. We know that teachers use proximity as a classroom management tool. Proximity also communicates value to students and the idea that they are psychologically close to the teacher. Teachers stand more often near students who perform well, students with whom they have a strong relationship. They also use proximity temporarily as a control when students are in trouble behaviorally. However, they consistently distance themselves from students they perceive as low achievers, albeit subconsciously.[8] When teachers change their proximity patterns, student learning can be positively impacted. Being at a close distance to students reinforces the idea that there is closeness in social and emotional ways as well. When teachers believe that students are low achieving, they[9]

- Get less wait time
- Are criticized more often for failure
- Are praised less frequently
- Receive less feedback
- Are called on less often
- Are seated farther away from the teacher
- Have less eye contact from the teacher
- Have fewer friendly interactions with the teacher
- Have their ideas accepted less often

QR Code 4.4:
Highlighting proximity
qrs.ly/79g86tx

Immediacy is a problem, but it is something that can be addressed with intentionality. In addition to moving around the classroom, teachers should consider the seating patterns that they use. In terms of seating patterns, lower-achieving students are typically placed (or are allowed to sit) in the back of the room or in the corners. On the other hand, students who have stronger relationships with the teacher are often found in the front and down the center of the room. This ***T-pattern***, the first two rows and the middle rows, is the group of students who tend to have the highest level of immediacy with the teacher. If this is happening, it needs to change. Of course, some students need to sit in the corners. It's a physics problem. But we encourage you to inventory which students are seated where and to make changes regularly so that you can minimize the impact of physical and emotional distance on students' learning.

VULNERABILITY

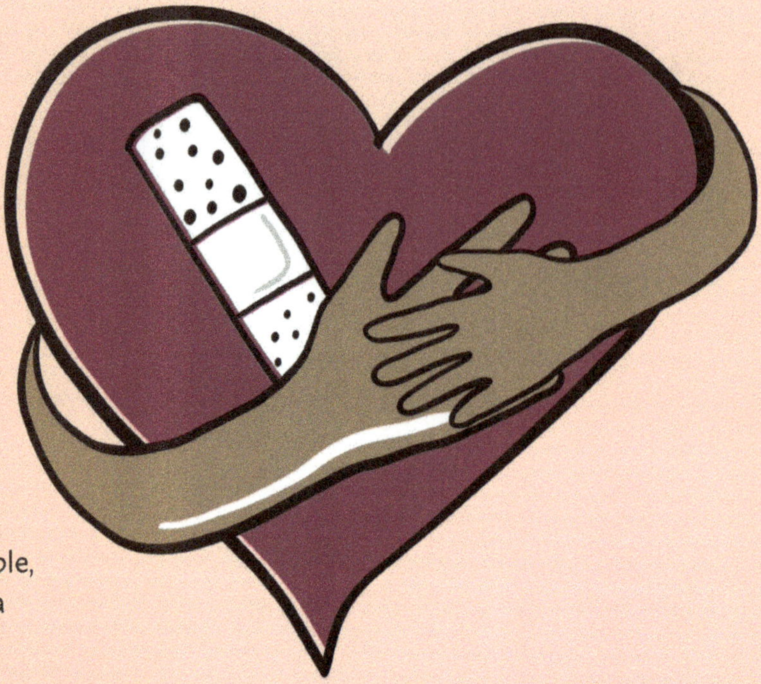

Others see us as available when we are vulnerable. Closeness develops when we are honest and acknowledge our weaknesses and insecurities. Having said that, you're still the teacher, and you deserve respect, but when you can make yourself vulnerable, take the opportunity. In fact, teaching is a "daily exercise in vulnerability."[10]

> *Vulnerability is the birthplace of love, belonging, joy, courage, empathy, and creativity. It is the source of hope, empathy, accountability, and authenticity. If we want greater clarity in our purpose or deeper and more meaningful spiritual lives, vulnerability is the path.*[11]

We are certainly not suggesting that teachers be weak. Instead, we hope that you engage in shared struggle and continuous exposure of the struggle. It means that you address your fears. It requires that you allow yourself to discover new things and learn new lessons. In essence, it means that you're comfortable opening up. And when you do, your immediacy with students grows. They feel closer to you and want to learn more. Take a risk and be vulnerable with your students. Start slowly but let them see that you are a complex person who has ups and downs. Let them know you a little more so that you develop the closeness that students crave from the adults who teach them. We promise, it will pay dividends.

QR Code 4.5: Teacher shares failure resume
qrs.ly/wbg86uo

THE POWER OF TOUCH

We could not end a discussion of immediacy without a discussion of physical contact with students. We recognize that many school systems have policies that prevent any hand shaking, high fives, or the like with students. We understand that this is an attempt to set limits and protect students. Yet we struggle with it. We are social animals, and touch conveys value and closeness.

Of course, there are cultural and gender boundaries, but the evidence on student achievement challenges assumptions about physical contact and suggests that many students respond to respectful touch.[12,13] The relationships that develop when teachers can shake the hand of a student entering the room, place a hand on a shoulder to communicate that they are doing a great job, or high five a student who has completed a major project are amazing. In addition, it should be noted that teachers can "touch" with their eyes and words—the wink of an eye for a job well done, a smile at the end of the presentation, and the use of pronouns such as *we* and *our* all communicate value and respect.

But if you are not comfortable with physical contact, be consistent. In other words, if you shake hands with some students, offer to shake hands with all students. As we have noted before, students are watching, and they notice when inequitable relationships develop. Students who are not greeted with a high five notice those who are and believe that they are less important to you.

QR Code 4.6: Focus on touch—handshakes and high fives
qrs.ly/s6g86u3

Notes on... IMMEDIACY

SECTION 5

ASSESSING YOUR CREDIBILITY

Now that you have come to the end of the book, we congratulate you on taking an interest in learning about credibility and taking the time to learn about ways you can strengthen your credibility with students. There are many ideas in the previous pages. We encourage you to think about the aspects of credibility that are already strengths for you and then consider one or two next best steps on things you could improve. Remember, teaching is a complex and overwhelming endeavor but comes with many rewards. Have a plan, take deliberate steps, and enlist the help of trusted mentors, coaches, and peers. We believe that you can do it and that you will realize significant benefits by engaging in this important development work.

Use the following self-assessment to identify your next steps in your teacher credibility journey.

TEACHER CREDIBILITY: SELF-ASSESSMENT

TRUSTWORTHINESS

ITEM #	SURVEY ITEM	Always	Sometimes	Rarely	Never
1.	When I make promises to students, I keep them, or I explain what happened if I cannot follow through.	3	2	1	0
2.	I am honest, but not hurtful, with students about their current performance levels.	3	2	1	0
3.	I implement strategies to repair trust when it is broken.	3	2	1	0
4.	I develop healthy, growth-producing relationships with students that create a climate where students can learn from mistakes and respect each other in learning.	3	2	1	0
5.	I ensure that I provide accurate, credible information to students.	3	2	1	0
Mean for Trustworthiness (Total divided by 5)					

COMPETENCE

ITEM #	SURVEY ITEM	Always	Sometimes	Rarely	Never
1.	My lessons are organized, and I use familiar strategies (or spend time teaching the new routines).	3	2	1	0
2.	I understand my content deeply and how to teach that content.	3	2	1	0
3.	I share learning intentions and success criteria with students for each lesson.	3	2	1	0
4.	I design and deliver quality instructional experiences aligned with what students need to know and be able to do.	3	2	1	0
5.	I seek and act on feedback from students, peers and leaders, and parents/guardians to improve the effectiveness of my teaching.	3	2	1	0
Mean for Competence (Total divided by 5)					

DYNAMISM

ITEM #	SURVEY ITEM	Always	Sometimes	Rarely	Never
1.	I bring passion and enthusiasm to the lessons I teach.	③	②	①	⓪
2.	I share the value of each lesson with students so that they understand the why of learning.	③	②	①	⓪
3.	When appropriate, I use personal stories, relevant and interesting videos, pictures, presentations, articles, etc. to make messages come alive for students.	③	②	①	⓪
4.	I carefully select independent learning tasks to maintain students' interest and their willingness to engage in meaningful practice.	③	②	①	⓪
5.	I am confident in my teaching, and it shows.	③	②	①	⓪
Mean for Dynamism (Total divided by 5)					

QR Code 5.1: Teacher reflects on credibility self-assessment qrs.ly/mag86u5

IMMEDIACY

ITEM #	SURVEY ITEM	Always	Sometimes	Rarely	Never
1.	My verbal and nonverbal communication signifies a genuine interest in others.	3	2	1	0
2.	I am intentional about being accessible and visible to students and parents/guardians.	3	2	1	0
3.	I enjoy being among students and sit with them at their tables and in their groups while they are working.	3	2	1	0
4.	I move around the room and am regularly within 3 feet of every student during the lesson.	3	2	1	0
5.	I start the class on time and use every minute wisely.	3	2	1	0
Mean for Immediacy (Total divided by 5)					

online resources Available for download at companion.corwin.com/courses/Teacher_Credibility

TAKE ACTION

Review all your action plans and your final self-assessment. What is your goal for teacher credibility? Which aspects are currently a strength for you or your team? What would you like to update?

Notes on...
DYNAMISM

APPENDIX

STUDENT TRUST IN FACULTY SCALE

Refer to **page 14** for the student survey.

SCORING INSTRUCTIONS

Step 1:

Calculate the average score for each survey participant by taking the mean of all 10 items of the Student Trust in Faculty scale.

Step 2:

Calculate the grand mean score on the Student Trust in Faculty scale for your school by taking an average of all the participants' individual scores.

Step 3:

Compute the Standardized Score for Student Trust in Faculty. In this step, you will convert your school's grand mean score to a standardized score with a mean of 500 and a standard deviation of 100, making comparison with other schools possible.

1. First compute the difference between your school's grand mean score on student trust in faculty (STF) and the mean for the normative sample. For a high school, this would mean (STF – 3.059).
2. Next, multiply the difference by one hundred [100(STF – 3.059)].
3. Divide the product by the standard deviation of the normative sample (0.728).
4. Add 500 to the result. You now have computed a standardized score: your Standardized Score for Student Trust in Faculty.

Use the appropriate formula below. Remember that the student trust survey has a 5-point response scale.

For high schools, calculate your standardized score using the following formula: Standardized Score for Student Trust in Faculty

(STF) = 100(STF – 3.059)/0.728 + 500 (as described above)

For middle schools, calculate your standardized trust score using the following formula: Standardized Score for Student Trust in Faculty

(STF) = 100(STF – 3.142)/0.861 + 500

For elementary schools, calculate your standardized trust score using the following formula: Standardized Score for Student Trust in Faculty

(STF) = 100(STF – 4.107)/0.781 + 500

The tool uses a mean of 500 and a standard deviation of 100, which allows you to create a standardized score and compare the scores of your classroom or school with those from a national sample. As noted by the authors, the range of the standardized scores is as follows:

- If the score is **200**, it is **lower than 99%** of the schools.
- If the score is **300**, it is **lower than 97%** of the schools.
- If the score is **400**, it is **lower than 84%** of the schools.
- If the score is **500**, it is **average**.
- If the score is **600**, it is **higher than 84%** of the schools.
- If the score is **700**, it is **higher than 97%** of the schools.
- If the score is **800**, it is **higher than 99%** of the schools.

Source: Adams & Forsyth (2009)

online resources Available for download at **companion.corwin.com/courses/Teacher_Credibility**

ENDNOTES

INTRODUCTION

1. Fisher, D., Frey, N., & Hattie, J. (2016). *Visible learning in literacy*. Corwin.
2. McCroskey, J. C., & Young, T. J. (1981). Ethos and credibility: The construct and its measurement after three decades. *Communication Studies, 32*, 24–34.

SECTION 1: TRUST

1. Hoy, W. K., & Tschannen-Moran, M. (2003). The conceptualization and measurement of faculty trust in schools: The omnibus T-Scale. In W. K. Hoy & C. G. Miskel (Eds.), *Studies in leading and organizing schools* (pp. 181–208). Information Age. (p. 189)
2. Baier, A. C. (1994). *Moral prejudices: Essays on ethics*. Harvard University Press. (p. 98)
3. von Frank, V. (2010). Trust matters—for educators, parents, and students. *Tools for Schools, 14*(1), 1–3.
4. Adams, C. M., & Forsyth, P. B. (2009). Conceptualizing and validating a measure of student trust. *Studies in School Improvement, 47*, 263–279.
5. Tschannen–Moran, M., & Barr, M. (2004). Fostering student learning: The relationship of collective teacher efficacy and student achievement. *Leadership and Policy in Schools, 3*(3), 189–209.
6. Marzano, R. J. (2011). Relating to students: It's what you do that counts. *Educational Leadership, 68*(6), 82–83. (p. 82)

SECTION 2: COMPETENCE

1. Banfield, S. R., Richmond, V. P., & McCroskey, J. C. (2006). The effect of teacher misbehaviors on teacher credibility and affect for the teacher. *Communication Education, 55*(1), 63–72. (p. 63)
2. Zeiger, S. (2018, June 18). *List of core competencies for educators.* https://work.chron.com/list-core-competencies-educators-8916.html
3. Shulman, L. S. (1986). Those who understand: Knowledge growth in teaching. *Educational Researcher, 15*, 4–14.
4. Fisher, D., Frey, N., & Hattie, J. (2016). *Visible learning in literacy*. Corwin.
5. Pearson, P. D., & Gallagher, G. (1983). The gradual release of responsibility model of instruction. *Contemporary Educational Psychology, 8*, 112–123.

SECTION 3: DYNAMISM

1. Wangberg, J. K. (1996). Teaching with a passion. *American Entomologist, 42*(4), 199–200. (p. 199)
2. Stuart, D. (2023). *The will to learn: Cultivating student motivation without losing your own*. Corwin.
3. Tate, M. (2015). *Worksheets don't grow dendrites: 20 instructional strategies that engage the brain* (3rd ed.). Corwin.
4. Gonzalez, J. (2016, March 26). *Frickin' packets.* https://www.cultofpedagogy.com/busysheets/
5. Poulou, M. S., Reddy, L. A., & Dudek, C. M. (2019). Relation of teacher self-efficacy and classroom practices: A preliminary investigation. *School Psychology International, 40*(1), 25–48.
6. Toropova, A., Myrberg, E., & Johansson, S. (2021). Teacher job satisfaction: The importance of school working conditions and teacher characteristics. *Educational Review, 73*(1), 71–79.
7. National Institute of Education. (2016). *Confident teachers make for confident learners.* https://singteach.nie.edu.sg/2016/03/10/issue56-research02/
8. Hasper, A. (2023, January 10). *4 tips for developing teacher confidence in the classroom.* https://teachingenglishwithoxford.oup.com/2023/01/10/tips-teacher-confidence/
9. Finley, T. (2023, September 12). *How teachers can build confidence.* https://www.edutopia.org/article/how-teachers-can-build-confidence/

10. Rosenberg, M. (1965). *Society and the adolescent self-image.* Princeton University Press.

11. Cottrell, D., & Harvey, E. (2004). *Leadership courage: Leadership strategies for individual and organizational success.* Walk the Talk Company.

SECTION 4: IMMEDIACY

1. Mehrabian, A. (1971). *Silent messages.* Wadsworth. (p. 1)

2. Andersen, J. A. (1979). Teacher immediacy as a predictor of teaching effectiveness. In B. D. Ruben (Ed.), *Annals of the International Communication Association Yearbook* (Vol. 3, pp. 543–559). Transaction Books.

3. Velez, J. J., & Cano, J. (2008). The relationship between teacher immediacy and student motivation. *Journal of Agricultural Education, 49*(3), 76–86.

4. Velez, J. J., & Cano, J. (2008). The relationship between teacher immediacy and student motivation. *Journal of Agricultural Education, 49*(3), 76–86. (p. 76)

5. Baringer, D. K., & McCroskey, J. C. (2000). Immediacy in the classroom: Student immediacy. *Communication Education, 49*(2), 178–186. (p. 178)

6. Richmond, V. P., McCroskey, J. C., & Johnson, A. D. (2003). Development of the nonverbal immediacy scale (NIS): Measures of self-and other-perceived nonverbal immediacy. *Communication Quarterly, 51*(4), 504–517.

7. Hess, J. A. (n.d.). *Effective instructional practices: Optimizing your immediacy.* National Communication Association. https://www.natcom.org/sites/default/files/pages/EIP_Optimizing_Your_Immediacy.pdf (p. 3)

8. Good, T. L. (1987). Two decades of research on teacher expectations. *Journal of Teacher Education, 38*, 32–47.

9. Good, T. L., Sterzinger, N., & Lavigne. A. L. (2018). Expectation effects: Pygmalion and the initial 20 years of research. *Educational Research and Evaluation, 24*(3–5), 99–123.

10. Palmer, P. (1998). *The courage to teach.* Jossey-Bass. (p. 17)

11. Brown, B. (2012). *Daring greatly: How the courage to be vulnerable transforms the way we live, love, parent, and lead.* Gotham. (p. 34)

12. Los Angeles County Office of Education. (2002). *Teacher expectations and student achievement.* Author.

13. El Hakim, S., & Danyal, F. (2024). From contact to connection: A comprehensive examination of affective touch in educational settings. *Frontiers in Psychology, 15.* doi:10.3389/fpsyg.2024.1230796

INDEX

ACO 365866